"ECHOES OF THE HEART"

APOORVA

Made with ❤ on the Notion Press Platform
www.notionpress.com

<u>*For My Family*</u>

This one is for you **Ma, Papa.**

Whose love and support have been the foundation of every word written here.

Contents

Contents

Foreword

When I first embarked on the journey of writing this collection, I had no idea where it would lead me. What started as a series of private reflections turned into a deeply personal exploration of the human heart. The poems within these pages are not merely words; *they are fragments of my soul, capturing moments of love, heartbreak, and the intricate tapestry of family bonds.*

Love is a universal experience, yet it is profoundly personal. Each relationship we encounter, whether fleeting or lifelong, leaves an indelible mark on our hearts. These poems share my experiences with love in different ways: the excitement of new romance, the deep sadness of loss, the strong bonds of family, and the simple beauty of everyday life.

Heartbreak, though painful, is an inevitable part of the human experience. It teaches us resilience, empathy, and the capacity for renewal. The poems about heartbreak in this book are a testament to the strength found in vulnerability and the hope that arises from healing.

Family, the cornerstone of our existence, shapes who we are. Through family, we learn our first lessons in love and trust. This collection pays homage to the familial relationships that have nurtured, challenged, and inspired me.

I invite you, dear reader, to delve into these poems with an open heart. Whether you find echoes of your own experiences or new perspectives, may these words bring you comfort, solace, and a deeper understanding of the intricate dance of human emotions.

Thank you for joining me on this journey. May you find as much joy in reading these poems as I saw in writing them.

With heartfelt gratitude,

Apoorva

Preface

Welcome to this collection of poems. These verses capture moments of love, heartbreak, and the bonds of family that have touched my life deeply. Each poem reflects personal experiences and emotions, exploring the highs of new love, the lows of loss, and the enduring strength found in family ties.

Writing these poems has been a journey of self-expression and discovery. Through these pages, I hope to share insights into the universal themes of love and relationships that resonate with us all. My wish is that these words resonate with your own experiences and emotions, offering comfort and connection in the shared human experience of love.

Thank you for exploring these poems with me. May they speak to your heart and remind you of the beauty and resilience found in every chapter of life.

Warm regards,

Apoorva

Acknowledgements

I am deeply grateful to everyone who has been a part of bringing this collection to life. Their support and encouragement have been invaluable throughout this creative journey.

First and foremost, I would like to thank [specific person or group] for their unwavering support and belief in my writing. Your encouragement kept me motivated during the moments of doubt.

I am also grateful to [mention individuals or organizations] for their constructive feedback and insights that helped refine these poems.

To my friends and family, thank you for your patience and understanding as I poured my heart into these pages. Your love and encouragement sustained me through the highs and lows of this endeavor.

Lastly, I extend my appreciation to my readers. Your interest in my work means the world to me, and I hope these poems resonate with you on a personal level.

Thank you all for being a part of this journey. Your support has made this dream a reality.

Prologue

TO GAMBLE

Welcome to this collection of poems, where emotions find voice in the cadence of words. These verses are a tapestry woven from moments of love, heartbreak, and the enduring ties of family.

"In this life, to live is to gamble in the emotions of fear, happiness, love, and anxiety—to make your soul strong and to bloom."

In these pages, you will discover reflections of personal journeys—of joyous beginnings and poignant endings, of resilience in the face of loss, and of the profound connections that shape our lives.

Each poem is a glimpse into the complexities of human experience, expressed through the lens of heartfelt emotions. As you embark on this poetic journey, I invite you to explore the depths of these emotions with an open heart.

May these poems resonate with you, offering solace, inspiration, and a deeper understanding of the shared threads that weave through our lives.

Warm regards,

Apoorva

1. TO LOVE

To love is to gamble, to risk, to dare,
To feel the joy, to face despair.
To love is to laugh and to cry,
To embrace the lows and touch the sky.
To love is to open your heart wide,
To be strong yet vulnerable inside.
To heal and to hurt, all in one,
To face the storm and greet the sun.
To love is to be yourself, yet more,
To become someone you adore.
To smile and give in ways so pure,
To find strength in love, that's for sure.

Though love is uncertain, wild, and free,
It helps us grow, to truly be.
To love is to flourish, to rise above,
For in the end, to love is to live and love.

2. TOGETHER

Dancing together in the rain,
Washing away all the pain.
I rest my head on his shoulder,
Feeling safe as we grow older.
His eyes, so shiny and bright,
Tease me softly in the light.
Holding hands, we walk the roads,
Sharing love that gently flows.
When he's weak, I hold him tight,
Being with him feels so right.
To be with him is to be home,
In his arms, I never roam.

He holds me close, we're never apart,
I pray to God with all my heart:
Let me be his place of peace,
Where he can rest and feel at ease.
No facades, just him and me,
Together, as we're meant to be.

3. HAPPINESS

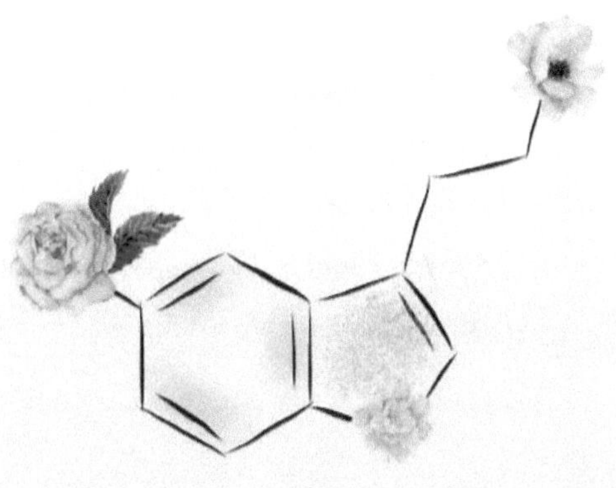

A smile is all we need to see,
A cherished hope that sets us free.
It never fades, it's always near,
A beacon bright that conquers fear.
We smile at flowers in full bloom,
Or dancing in the rainy gloom.
Happiness, like the rising sun,
A rainbow bright when rain is done.

Happiness is holding dear,
Those we love, so close, so near.
A knitted bond, a warm embrace,
Brings a smile to light our face.
When our favorite dish is made,
Or street food on a busy parade.
Reading books that bring delight,
A smile that shines so pure and bright.
So let's treasure every day,
With smiles that light our way.
For happiness is all around,
In simple joys, it's always found.

4. FRIENDSHIP

Friendship is a precious gem,
A bond that shines, a vibrant stem.
Through thick and thin, it's always there,
A loyal heart, a love to share.
We laugh together, tears we dry,
With friends beside us, we can fly.
In joy and sorrow, day and night,
Friendship's glow is warm and bright.

We share our dreams, our hopes, our fears,
Together through the fleeting years.
In simple moments, grand and small,
A friend's embrace can heal it all.
Adventures bold, or quiet days,
With friends, we find a million ways.
To smile, to grow, to understand,
To lend a comforting, helping hand.
So here's to friends, both near and far,
Our guiding light, our northern star.
In friendship's warmth, we find our way,
A cherished gift, come what may.

5. FAMILY

Family is the heart's own song,
A bond that's cherished, deep and strong.
Through every trial, joy, and pain,
In family, love will always reign.
In laughter shared and tears we cry,
Together, we reach for the sky.
In darkest nights and brightest days,
Family guides us through life's maze.

The hugs that mend a broken heart,
The words of love that never part.
In every quarrel, every fight,
Family holds us through the night.
With parents' wisdom, siblings' cheer,
We face our fears, we persevere.
Grandparents' stories, old and wise,
Light up our hearts and clear our eyes.
The table set for meals so grand,
The touch of a comforting hand.
In family, we find our place,
A circle bound by love and grace.
When the world is harsh and cold,
Family's warmth we tightly hold.
In every smile, in every tear,
Family's love is always near.
Through all of life, its ups and downs,
In family, our strength abounds.
A legacy of love, so true,
In family, we find our hue.

6. RAIN'S SONG

The drops of rain, like soft guitar,
Whispers speaking from afar.
They dance upon the earth so free,
A song of joy, for you and me.
In the rain, I lose myself,
Finding happiness, like hidden wealth.
Each drop a note, a gentle rhyme,
Bringing peace in rhythm and time.

Pitter-patter, soothing sound,
Like a lullaby, safe and sound.
It eases worries, calms our mind,
Leaving all our troubles behind.
Dark clouds may come, shadows near,
But raindrops fall, washing clear.
They cleanse our hearts, wash away,
All our doubts, on rainy day.
The smell of rain, fresh and clean,
Underneath the sky's vast screen.
It fills our souls with love and light,
Making everything feel right.
So let the rain fall, soft and true,
A song of peace, just for you.
In its embrace, we find our way,
Rain's gentle song, every day.

7. HEART BREAK

I smile, concealing the pain deep inside,
The sound of heartbreak, silent, I hide.
I pave my way, a facade so bright,
But I cry alone in the dead of night.
It's like I'm suffocating with each breath I take,
Yet I smile, a light, for everyone's sake.
Working, driving aimlessly through the days,
Distracting myself, or I'll fade away.

I navigate life, lost in a daze,
Hoping distractions will blur this maze.
But in quiet moments, the sorrow seeps,
A hidden river where my heart weeps.
Each laugh, a mask, each word, a shield,
Protecting wounds that never healed.
For in the night, when I'm alone,
I face the truth I've never shown.
This heartbreak echoes in my chest,
A silent storm that grants no rest.
Yet I smile, and move, and strive,
Finding ways to stay alive.

8. MOVING ON

I type the letter of a breaking bond,
While caring, forcing myself to stay strong.
I smile when people call me a cheat,
Unaware of the story beneath my heartbeat.
I can't move on, but I have to try,
I can't leave these feelings, though I must comply.
It's like a story so beautiful and bright,
That I break myself, smiling wide in the night.

Each word I write, a fragment of pain,
Yet I hold it together in the pouring rain.
The whispers, the judgments, they don't know me,
They don't see the heartbreak or the silent plea.
I carry this burden, heavy and deep,
In the daylight, I laugh, but at night, I weep.
A tale of love that's now a ghost,
Haunting my heart, the one I loved most.
Yet onward I go, with a facade of grace,
Hiding the cracks, the tears on my face.
For in this act of letting go,
I find the strength to slowly grow.

9. TEARS

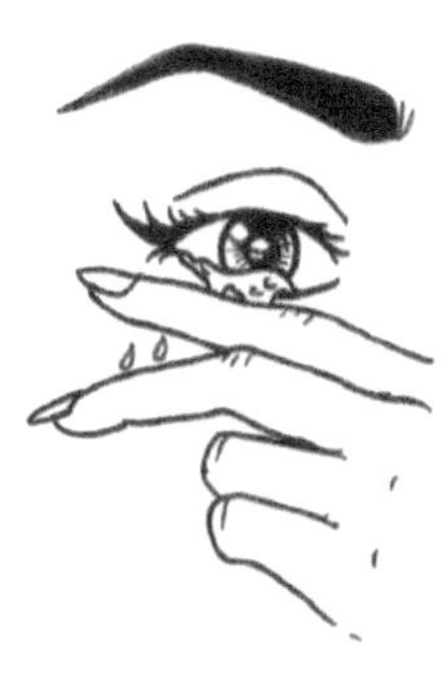

Tears, they fall like gentle rain,
A silent testament to hidden pain.
Each drop, a story untold,
A piece of heartache, a soul consoled.
In their shimmer, reflections lie,
Of laughter lost and whispered goodbyes.
They trace the contours of a weary face,
Leaving trails of sorrow and grace.
Tears of joy, when hearts unite,
Glimmer in the softest light.
Tears of loss, when love departs,

Cascade from the depths of broken hearts.
In every tear, a world unfolds,
A tale of courage, a hand to hold.
They cleanse the spirit, wash the strife,
Bringing solace, renewing life.
So let them fall, these human tears,
In moments of triumph, in times of fears.
For they are the language of the soul,
Making the broken beautifully whole.

10. THRONY ROSE

In gardens where roses grow,
A story unfolds that we all know.
With beauty blooming, petals fair,
Yet hidden thorns, they linger there.
Soft to touch, yet sharp within,
A contrast where joy and pain begin.
For every joy that roses bring,

A hidden thorn may prick and sting.
So admire roses, lovely and bright,
But beware the thorns, hidden from sight.
In their beauty, a lesson shows,
That even roses bear both highs and lows.

11. THE POISON WE CHOOSE

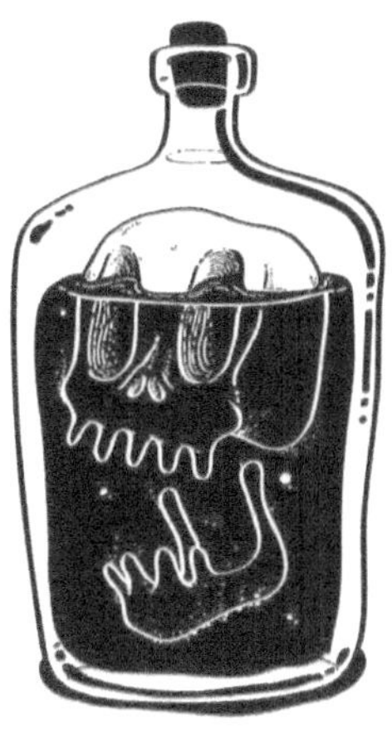

We drink the poison our minds serve us,
Not knowing why it makes us ill thus.
Lost in our choices, blind and unclear,
Drinking illusions, ignoring what's near.
It tastes sweet at first, a fleeting delight,
But its harm spreads fast, out of sight.
We wonder why sickness takes its toll,

Unaware we're consuming poison whole.
Each sip seems tempting, a dangerous game,
A toxic path, leading us to shame.
As darkness falls, we question our fate,
Yet keep drinking poison, tempting our state.
In our minds, the poison resides,
While the cure we need, we push aside.
In the end, the choice is our own,
To stop drinking poison, or let it be known.

12. FEAR OF HONESTY

Some days, fear grips my pen,
Afraid that honesty will condemn.
Words unsaid weigh heavy, deep,
Their truth a wound that doesn't sleep.
In silence, safety I may find,
But truths unspoken haunt my mind.
Honesty cuts, sharp as a knife,
Revealing truths that alter life.

Yet silence, too, has its cost,
Leaving hearts and souls lost.
So I write, despite the fear,
To face the truths that linger near.
For honesty, though it may sting,
Can also heal, like a gentle spring.
In words laid bare, a chance to see,
The truth that sets my spirit free.

13. STRENGTH IN SOLITUDE

On my own, I found my way,
Learning to be strong day by day.
No family, friends, or love in sight,
But within myself, I found my light.
Through tough times when no one's near,
I stood tall, overcoming fear.
Though support was far, I carried on,
Discovering strength, from dusk to dawn.

In solitude's embrace, I learned to thrive,
Finding power in being alive.
No hand to hold, no shoulder to lean,
Yet I found the courage to chase my dream.
Through loneliness, I grew strong and bold,
Realizing resilience, mine to hold.
In the end, all on my own,
I learned that strength was always home.

14. SILENT REFLECTION

There are moments when silence surrounds me,
No words can capture what my heart can see.
In the quiet depths of my mind's embrace,
Emotions swirl, leaving traces I can't erase.
I stay silent, not because I don't care,
But because words fail to convey what's there.
Feelings too complex, thoughts too deep,
In the silence, they find a place to sleep.

My heart whispers secrets, my mind spins tales,
In silence, I navigate these emotional gales.
No need for words to justify or explain,
Sometimes silence speaks more than refrain.
For in the stillness, I find clarity,
Understanding the depths of my reality.
Silent but not lost, I listen and learn,
In the stillness, emotions burn.
So I embrace the silence, where no words are found,
Knowing that within, truths abound.
Sometimes, in the stillness, I find my way,
Navigating emotions, come what may.

15. FACING REALITY

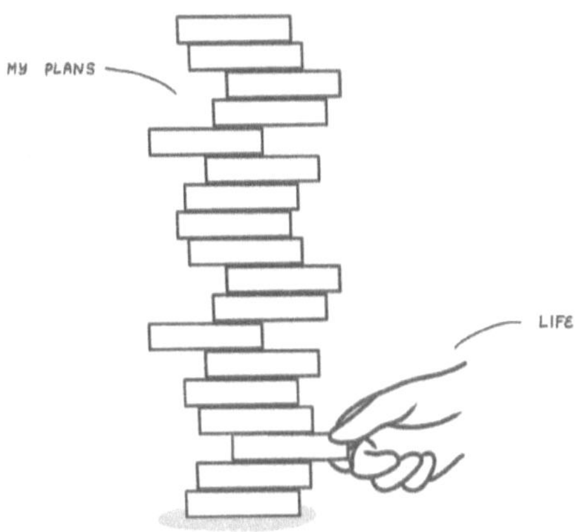

I convince myself I need nobody near,
Yet deep down, the truth becomes clear.
Nobody needs me, that's what I say,
Alone in the silence, day by day.
It's a bitter truth, hard to ignore,
Feeling unwanted, left at the door.
In solitude's grip, I wrestle alone,
Longing for a place to call my own.

But amidst the loneliness, a spark remains,
A glimmer of hope amidst the pains.
For in the quiet, I find my strength,
Reclaiming worth, regardless of length.
Though it seems nobody needs me now,
I'll find my way, somehow, somehow.
For self-worth blooms not from others' gaze,
But in the heart's resilience, through endless days.

16. IMAGINERY HAPPINESS

When alone, I turn to my mind,
Creating joy that's hard to find.
With eyes closed tight, I start to see,
A world where happiness comes to me.
In my thoughts, I build a place,
Where smiles bloom on every face.

I imagine laughter, warm and bright,
Chasing away the darkest night.
Though real life might sometimes be tough,
In my mind, I've had enough.
I escape to where dreams are free,
And happiness is all I see.
So when the world feels cold and gray,
I close my eyes and drift away.
In my imagination's gentle embrace,
I find the warmth of a happy space.

17. QUITE LOVE

In my heart, feelings run deep,
Simple words, yet secrets I keep.
Love for you, quietly I hold,
Emotions strong, yet never told.
With every breath, with every sigh,
My love for you, I can't deny.
Though silent, it's as deep as the sea,
A cherished bond, just you and me.
In the quiet moments, my heart sings,
Longing for the touch your presence brings.
Simple words, but emotions strong,
In my heart, you truly belong.

18. HIM

He resides in her thoughts, a constant refrain,
A melody that echoes through joy and pain.
Like a song she can't forget, he plays on repeat,
Each note a memory, bittersweet.
In the quiet hours, his voice softly sings,
Echoes of laughter and tender things.
She tries to move on, but he's always near,
His presence a comfort, yet also a fear.
His words linger in her mind, clear as day,
A haunting tune she can't push away.

Like a melody etched in her soul,
His presence fills every empty hole.
She wonders if he hears her heart's plea,
The unspoken words she longs to set free.
For he's not just a song, but a part of her soul,
A melody that continues to console.
Though she tries to drown out his song,
In her heart, his melody remains strong.
For he's woven into her story, deep and true,
A song she can't forget, no matter what she'll do.

19. TO BE FOUND

At times, it feels like vanishing is the answer,
But deep down, it's about wanting someone to discover.
It's not about fading into the dark,
But rather, longing for someone to leave a mark.
Yearning for recognition, not invisibility,
Seeking connection, not solitude's ability.
In the quiet corners of the mind, this truth is found,
Desiring to be seen, in silence, without a sound.
So, in moments of seeming disappearance,
Remember, it's about seeking existence's reassurance.
To be recognized, understood, and loved,

APOORVA

For who we are, in this vast world, beloved.

20. BLAMING MYSELF

I turned out to be a horrible person.
and I have no-one to blame

but myself

In the quiet of my thoughts, I often find,
A familiar echo, an accusing kind.
"It's always my fault," whispers the voice,
Leaving me questioning, with no other choice.
Through trials and troubles, I bear the weight,
Blaming myself, accepting my fate.
Every misstep, every stumble, every fall,
I'm quick to blame, feeling small.
But deep down, I know it's not true,
Fault isn't always mine to accrue.
Life's complexities, its twists and turns,

Not solely my burden, not solely my concerns.
So I'll silence that voice, stand up tall,
Realize it's okay to sometimes fall.
Fault may come, but it's not always mine,
In the grand tapestry of life's design.

21. RIGHT OR WRONG

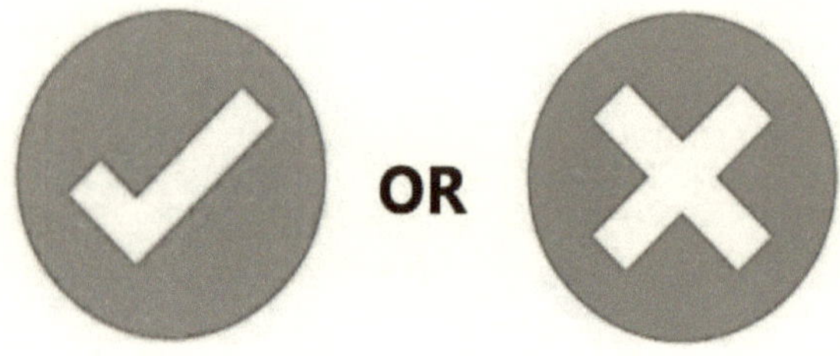

Have you ever felt like every choice you made was right,
Yet somehow, everything still turned to night?
In the quiet moments, questioning your path,
Wondering how good intentions led to aftermath.
You followed your heart, trusted your gut,
Yet outcomes twisted, leaving you in a rut.
Confusion reigns, doubts begin to creep,
As if clarity evades you, while you're asleep.
But maybe right and wrong aren't so clear,
Life's complexities, the shadows they steer.

Sometimes, despite our best intents,
Fate takes its own course, leaving us in suspense.
So hold onto faith, through the storm and through,
Know that every effort was true.
In the face of doubt, stand strong and fight,
For even when it's dark, there's always light.

22. THE LIGHT OF KINDNESS

People who wait while you tie your shoes,
In their patience, a silent, gentle muse.
People who shift closer as you move away,
In their presence, a comfort that wants to stay.
People who smile when you meet their eye,
In their warmth, a promise, no need to ask why.
People who seek you to share good news,
In their joy, a bond that feels like a muse.

People who listen, who truly hear,
In their understanding, a love that's clear.
People who stand by, through thick and thin,
In their loyalty, a strength within.
People who laugh with you, cry with you too,
In their emotions, a friendship true.
People who hold you when the world feels cold,
In their embrace, a story unfolds.
People who notice the little things,
In their awareness, a harmony sings.
People who share your dreams and fears,
In their presence, the future appears.
People who lift you when you're feeling low,
In their encouragement, a love that grows.
People who celebrate every success,
In their cheers, a happiness.
These are the souls who make life bright,
In their kindness, we find our light.
For in their eyes, we see the proof,
That in this world, love is the truth.

23. CONFUSING SCILENCE

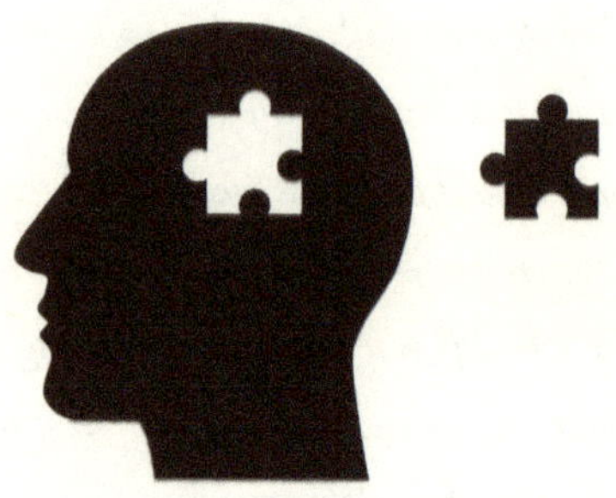

Why can't you tell me what you feel?
Your silence keeps me from what is real.
Because how you act is confusing me,
A maze of emotions, hard to see.
You smile, you laugh, yet drift away,
In your actions, I lose my way.
Your words are few, your thoughts concealed,
In this quiet, no truth revealed.
I search your eyes for hidden signs,
For whispered truths between the lines.

Yet all I find is mystery,
A heart that's locked, no clear decree.
Why can't you tell me what's inside?
In your silence, my hope's denied.
Because how you act leaves me guessing,
In your presence, my heart's confessing.
I long for words to break this spell,
For honesty where secrets dwell.
So speak to me, let your heart be seen,
In truth and love, let us convene.

24. PATHS

People come and go; that's what is life,
In fleeting moments, joy and strife.
Faces change, and names may fade,
In the dance of time, our paths are laid.
Some bring laughter, bright and clear,
Others bring lessons, sharp and severe.
In their passing, memories stay,
Echoes of yesterday, guiding our way.

Like leaves that drift on autumn's breeze,
We move through life with gentle ease.
Connections form, then slip away,
In the ebb and flow of each new day.
Yet each encounter leaves a mark,
A trace of light in the deepest dark.
For in the coming and the going,
We find ourselves, forever growing.
So cherish those who cross your path,
In their presence, find your hearth.
For people come and people go,
That's what makes this life we know.

25. STRENGTH IN SCARS

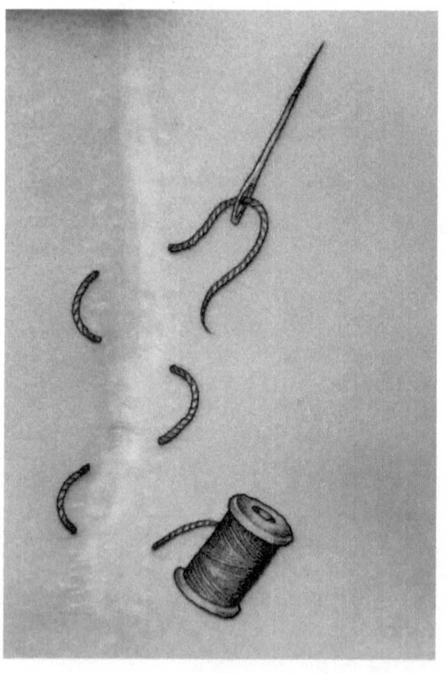

Damaged wings train you to fly,
Better than healed ones ever could try.
In the struggle and the pain,

Lessons learned, strength we gain.
Each tear, each scar, a story told,
Of battles fought and courage bold.
In the face of storms we rise,
With wisdom shining in our eyes.
For broken wings still find the sky,
In their resilience, they defy.
The limits set by past defeat,
In every fall, they find their feet.
Healed wings may forget the fight,
The darkest days, the endless night.
But damaged wings, they hold the key,
To soaring high, wild and free.
Embrace the scars, the wounds that burn,
In their fire, new strength we earn.
For damaged wings, though frail they seem,
Hold the power to chase the dream.
So fly with wings both torn and mended,
In their beauty, strength extended.
For in the broken, lies the grace,
To find the light, to find our place.

26. LEAVE THE RAIN BEHIND

Whatever causes rain in your soul,
And the pain that takes its toll,
Leave it behind, let it go,
Find the light, let your spirit glow.
In every tear, a story lies,
Of broken dreams and silent cries.
Yet in the heart, a strength unknown,
A will to rise, to stand alone.
The clouds may gather, dark and dense,
Shrouding joy with their pretense.

But within you, a fire burns bright,
A beacon in the darkest night.
Let go of sorrow, shed the weight,
Step into a brighter fate.
For in the leaving, freedom's found,
In silent peace, without a sound.
Whatever causes rain to fall,
Release its grip, stand tall.
For in the clearing of the skies,
A new dawn waits, a fresh sunrise.
So chase the storms away with grace,
Find your joy in a new place.
Leave the pain and rain behind,
In love and hope, new strength you'll find.

27. DESTINED PATH

If it's meant to be, it will be,
A path unfolding, wild and free.
In the tapestry of fate's design,
Threads of destiny intertwine.
Through twists and turns, we journey on,
In the rising light of each new dawn.
Challenges come, and trials test,

Yet in the journey, we find rest.
For what is meant will find its way,
In the rhythm of night and day.
Trust in the timing, trust in the flow,
Letting go of what we cannot know.
In moments still, and dreams so grand,
In the touch of fate's gentle hand.
If it's meant to heal, it will mend,
In the echoes of a heart on the mend.
For love and life, in harmony,
In the dance of possibility.
If it's meant to soar, it will fly,
In the boundless reach of the open sky.
So hold on tight, yet let it be,
In the grace of what is meant to be.
For in the whispers of the soul's decree,
Lies the truth of our destiny.

28. FOREVER IS JUST MEMORIES

forever...

Maybe forever was a word
Meant for memories, not people heard.
In the tapestry of time, they weave,
Moments cherished, hearts believe.
For people come and people go,
In the ebb and flow, the highs and low.
But memories linger, soft and clear,
In the whispers of the heart, they're near.
Forever found in laughter shared,
In the love that showed how much we cared.

Though people part, and paths diverge,
In memories, they forever surge.
For maybe forever was never meant
To bind us to each passing event.
But to live on in the stories we tell,
In the echoes of a love that dwells.
So let us hold onto memories bright,
In their warmth, find solace in the night.
For maybe forever finds its place,
In the memories we forever embrace.

29. GRATEFUL FOR MEMORIES

Thank you for all the memories we've shared,
In my heart, they're cherished and cared.
From the laughter that echoed in the air,
To the moments of joy we were happy to share.

Thank you for the times we laughed till we cried,
For the adventures where our spirits soared high.
Through ups and downs, thick and thin,
You were there, a true friend and kin.
Thank you for the late-night talks and deep conversations,
For the comfort found in silent contemplations.
In those quiet moments, we understood each other's hearts,
We found solace in our unspoken parts.
Thank you for the celebrations, big and small,
For the milestones we marked, standing tall.
Each memory a thread in life's tapestry,
Painting a picture of our shared journey.
Thank you for the lessons learned,
Through challenges faced and bridges burned.
For in those trials, we grew strong,
Learning together where we belong.
Thank you for the memories that make me smile,
For the warmth they bring across the miles.
They remind me of the bonds we've made,
Of the love that never seems to fade.
Thank you for being there, my friend,
For the support that never seems to end.
In gratitude, I hold these memories dear,
For they remind me of why I'm glad you're here.

30. FEAR OF LOOSING YOU

thantophobia

(n.) the phobia of losing
someone you love

Why am I afraid to lose you,
When you were never mine to hold true?
Your presence fills my heart and mind,
Yet the fear of loss is unkind.
In dreams and thoughts, you're always there,
A bond unseen, beyond compare.
But in reality's cold embrace,
I fear losing you without a trace.
It's the connection we share, so deep,
That makes me afraid to let go, to weep.
For in my heart, you've found a place,

And losing you would leave an empty space.
Though you're not mine to claim as mine,
The thought of losing you feels like a sign.
A reminder of what could have been,
Leaving me lost in a world so keen.
So I hold on to the moments we share,
In silence, in dreams, in quiet despair.
Hoping that one day, you'll be mine,
Until then, I fear losing you, undefined.